The Technology of Farming

Producing Fish

Barbara A. Somervill

Chicago, Illinois

www.capstonepub.com
Visit our website to find out more information about Heinemann-Raintree books.

To order:
☎ Phone 888-454-2279
💻 Visit www.capstonepub.com to browse our catalog and order online.

Edited by Abby Colich, Megan Cotugno, and Nancy Dickmann
Designed by Victoria Allen
Picture research by Elizabeth Alexander
Illustrations by Oxford Designers and Illustrators

Originated by Capstone Global Library Ltd
Printed and bound in China by China Translation and Printing Services Ltd

16 15 14 13 12
10 9 8 7 6 5 4 3 2 1

Library of Congress Cataloging-in-Publication Data
Somervill, Barbara A.
  Producing fish / Barbara A. Somervill.—1st ed.
    p. cm.—(The technology of farming)
  Includes bibliographical references and index.
  ISBN 978-1-4329-6405-4 (hb)—ISBN 978-1-4329-6412-2 (pb)
1. Fish culture—Juvenile literature. 2. Fishing—Juvenile literature. I. Title. II. Series: Technology of farming.
  SH151.S66 2012
  664'.94—dc23   2011037496

Acknowledgments
We would like to thank the following for permission to reproduce photographs: Alamy: pp. 9 (© www.BibleLandPictures.com), 11 (© Pat Canova), 21 (© Accent Alaska.com), 27 (© Stephen Frink Collection), 34 (© Peter Titmuss); Corbis: pp. 5 (© Jeffrey Rotman), 10 (© Alfredo Dagli Orti/The Art Archive), 15 (© Hein van den Heuvel), 28 (© Bojan Brecelj), 41 (© Joel W. Rogers); FLPA: p. 39 (Norbert Wu/Minden Pictures); Getty Images: pp. 7 (Christopher Furlong), 16 (Paul Sutherland/National Geographic), 23 (HOANG DINH NAM/AFP), 26 (Jeff J Mitchell), 31 (Randy Olson/National Geographic), 33 (Olivier Morin/AFP), 37 (Stockbyte), 43 (Barcroft USA); Mary Evans Picture Library: p. 13; Photolibrary: p. 25 (MIXA Co. Ltd.); Science Photo Library: p. 8 (Sheila Terry); Shutterstock: pp. 6 (© Gordon Warlow), 19 (© holbox), 22 left (© saiko3p), 22 right (© Alex Staroseltsev), 35 (© T.W. van Urk).

Cover photo of a man working in a fish processing plant reproduced with permission from Photolibrary (Kristjan Maack/Nordic Photos).

Every effort has been made to contact copyright holders of any material reproduced in this book. Any omissions will be rectified in subsequent printings if notice is given to the publisher.

Disclaimer
All the Internet addresses (URLs) given in this book were valid at the time of going to press. However, due to the dynamic nature of the Internet, some addresses may have changed, or sites may have changed or ceased to exist since publication. While the author and publisher regret any inconvenience this may cause readers, no responsibility for any such changes can be accepted by either the author or the publisher.

Contents

Some words appear in the text in bold, **like this**. You can find out what they mean by looking in the glossary.

Can We Have Fish for Dinner?

Around the world, fishing **vessels** work at sea each day. They catch the fish and seafood that ends up on our dinner tables. The vessels may be small and haul in shrimp, crabs, or lobsters. They may be the size of a small factory. Factory ships catch, process, package, and freeze fish fresh from the ocean. The work is hard. The weather is often miserable.

Fishing

The sea provides mystery, danger, and a bounty of food. The general term for harvesting that food is fishing. Fishing covers finfish, such as tuna, swordfish, and salmon. Fishers also catch shellfish, such as clams, oysters, and mussels. They capture crustaceans, including shrimp and lobsters. Other products of the sea that fall under fishing include whales and seals, which are marine mammals; sea turtles, which are reptiles; and octopus and squid, which are mollusks.

Depending on the species of fish or shellfish, fishing can be a seasonal event. Salmon, for example, live their adult lives in the ocean until it is time to reproduce. The salmon then return to the freshwater stream where they hatched. Salmon fishers wait for the few weeks in the spring when they are allowed to catch wild salmon. The catch is sold fresh, frozen, canned, and smoked. In many countries, smoked salmon is a delicacy served only on special occasions.

This fisher in Massachusetts has made a good-sized catch of flounder, cod, and lobster.

The freshest fish

Because Japan is an island nation, the Japanese people eat a great deal of seafood. They stir-fry fish, shrimp, or crab with vegetables and serve it with rice. They also eat sushi and sashimi. Sushi is cold, cooked rice served with raw fish. Sashimi is raw fish served in small bite-sized pieces that are dipped in soy sauce and horseradish.

Only a skilled chef earns the right to be called a sushi master. Sushi chefs learn how to choose the finest, freshest fish. They precisely carve tender morsels into appealing shapes. In sushi restaurants around the world, people feast on raw shrimp, tuna, squid, and even octopus. Since the fish is raw, diners need to know they are eating the freshest possible fish.

Sushi chefs shop fish markets as early as 4:00 a.m. to find the perfect fish for top-quality sushi.

Traditional fish and chips is served wrapped in a sheet of paper.

Family favorite

On the streets of coastal towns around the world, people bite into a popular treat—fish-and-chips. "Chips" is the British term for French fries, and fish-and-chips is a popular food in the United Kingdom. A fillet of fish such as cod or haddock is battered and deep-fried. Fish-and-chips is served around the world, although the fish species may change. Beside Australia's Botany Bay or in the streets of New Zealand's Christchurch, the fish is more likely to be bream or flathead. In San Francisco and Vancouver, fish-and-chips shops serve up halibut or pollock. Regardless of the species of fish used, this dish is a favorite of many.

When Did People First Start Fishing?

Neanderthals were early relatives of humans who emerged over 100,000 years ago and died out over 24,000 years ago. Scientists studied the bones of Neanderthals that lived beside oceans or seas. They found chemicals in Neanderthal bones that show that these people ate large quantities of fish, shellfish, and marine mammals.

The Neanderthals dumped shells and bones in a garbage heap called a **midden**. Scientists have also found **evidence** that these early humans went on seasonal fishing trips.

This illustration shows early humans using a canoe and net to catch fish.

Neanderthals may not have been the first human fishers. They did, however, develop successful fishing skills to feed their **clans**. They made spears from long shafts of wood. They formed spearheads from sharp stone. Spearing a fish required practice and skill.

Catching small fish was hard to do with a spear. By about 8000 BCE, humans began fishing with hooks made from animal bones. They made lines by weaving fibers from **flax** or wool together. Hook-and-line fishing proved successful, but it was hard to catch enough fish to feed many people.

Fishhooks

People began making fishhooks from copper and bronze around 4000 BCE. Ancient copper hooks have been found in Crete, Italy, and the Indus Valley of northern India. As people learned how to use iron, around 800 to 200 BCE, blacksmiths began forging iron fishhooks. Strong, larger iron hooks allowed fishers to catch much larger fish.

Fishhooks such as this one were used in Ancient Rome.

Fish for many

Using nets for fishing was the next **technological** advance. Nets allowed one or two people to catch enough fish for an entire clan. People wove nets using grasses, wool, or flax. Stones weighted the bottoms of the nets. This allowed people to drag the nets along riverbeds or in shallow coastal water to scoop up fish.

Fish farming began in China around the 400s BCE during the Zhou dynasty. Fish farmers collected young species of carp, including goldfish and koi, from local streams and raised them in ponds. Farming fish was also common in ancient Egypt during the Middle Kingdom (2040–1633 BCE). In 30 BCE Rome invaded Egypt, which was when Romans learned about fish farming. Both Egyptians and Romans farmed several types of fish and also raised oyster beds.

Early Egyptian people fished the Nile River with handheld nets.

Shellfish leave a trail

Throughout the world, many people who lived along rivers and coasts ate clams, mussels, marine mammals, and crabs. These foods are not fish, but they are harvested from the sea. People tossed the leftover shells in garbage piles, called middens. Middens have lasted many thousands of years and may measure several miles long and tens of feet high. Scientists can figure out how old a midden is from the shells and bones at the bottom. Humans started the earliest middens several thousand years ago.

A midden like this depiction of one shows that an entire village ate clams on a regular basis.

Whaling

Whales are not fish. They are marine mammals that are hunted in the world's oceans. The process of hunting whales is called whaling. The earliest whalers set to sea in small one- or two-person boats. They herded whales toward the shore, making loud noises. If a whale beached itself, the hunt was a success. This technique was used in the North Pacific Ocean and North Atlantic Ocean.

As whaling advanced, the Ainu of Japan, Inuit of North America, and Basques of Spain began using **drogues** when whaling. Whalers speared a whale using a **harpoon**, and the whale dragged the drogue, a floating weight, until it tired. Then the whale was killed and towed to shore.

In the early 1600s, whalers from Amsterdam in the Netherlands and San Sebastian, Spain, traveled north in the Atlantic Ocean in large ships. They caught whales and processed the blubber into whale oil at sea. The whalers returned to port with cargo holds full of oil. This was the beginning of **commercial** whaling.

Uses for whale products

People found many uses for whale products. Whale oil burned in lamps at night. Many European women wore corsets (a type of undergarment) strengthened with whalebone and styled their hair with whalebone combs. Whale oil was also used in making soaps and paint. Sperm whales provided spermaceti (a waxy material) for making candles and ambergris, an ingredient in perfume. Craftspeople carved whale teeth into piano keys and chess pieces.

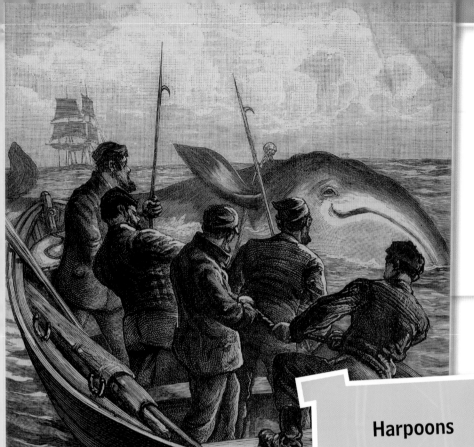

This illustration from the 1800s shows whalers on a small boat using harpoons to catch a whale.

For more than 300 years, whaling **vessels** harvested whales, until many species were nearly **extinct**. In 1986 most International Whaling Commission members agreed to stop commercial whaling. Despite this agreement, Japan, Iceland, and Norway continue to hunt whales for meat. Some American Indian groups are still legally allowed to hunt whales.

Harpoons

For more than 8,000 years, whalers used harpoons to catch whales. A harpoon has a sharp spearhead with a **barbed** end and a long wooden shaft. A rope is attached to the shaft like a fishing line is attached to a rod and reel. The harpoon is thrown like a spear and sticks into the whale's flesh. Today harpoons are shot from powerful guns mounted on the deck of a whaling vessel.

What Is Commercial Fishing?

Commercial fishing, also called capture fishing, is the business of catching and selling fish for **profit**. Commercial fishing **vessels** may be large or small. A small fishing vessel measures about 40 feet (12 meters) long. A vessel that catches and processes its catch on board can be 170 feet (52 meters) long or larger. They may fish close to shore or in the deep ocean.

Fishing vessels are designed to do specific types of fishing. A ship that catches shrimp, for example, would not be good for catching tuna. The place where the fish or shellfish are caught is called a **fishery**. There are tuna fisheries, for example, in the Atlantic, Pacific, and Indian oceans.

Fifty-four percent of commercial fishers **trawl** for their catches. Trawlers have large nets that they drag behind them. The nets, called trawls, are shaped like funnels with a wide opening at the front and a closed end, called the cod end. As the ship moves forward, fish are trapped in the net. Trawling is commonly used for catching anchovies, cod, squid, and shrimp.

International Council for the Exploration of the Sea

Based in Copenhagen, Denmark, the International Council for the Exploration of the Sea (ICES) is the oldest international organization for studying marine resources. ICES is a network of more than 1,600 scientists and 200 institutes. They offer advice about fishing species at risk of becoming **extinct**.

Trawlers pull large, bag-shaped nets behind or to the side of them to collect fish.

Purse seine

A **purse seine** is a fishing net with rings along the bottom and floats along the top. The net is like a long fence dropped in the water. A line is passed through the bottom rings. When the net is full of fish, the line is pulled tight, and the fish are caught. About one-fourth of all commercial fishers use purse seines.

A large purse seine can catch as much as 400 tons (363 metric tons) of fish at one time. Small-**gauge** nets are used for sardines and anchovies. Larger-gauge nets haul in salmon and some types of tuna.

This purse seine surrounds a school of southern bluefin tuna.

Longlines

A **longline** is a central fishing line that can range from 1 to 50 miles (1.6 to 80 kilometers) long. Shorter lines, called snoods, dangle from the central line and have baited hooks on the end. Longlines trail behind a vessel and are used to catch tuna or swordfish. The lines may also be attached to anchors for catching fish that live close to the seafloor, such as halibut. One serious problem about longlines is that they can also catch sea turtles, sharks, and seabirds, such as albatrosses.

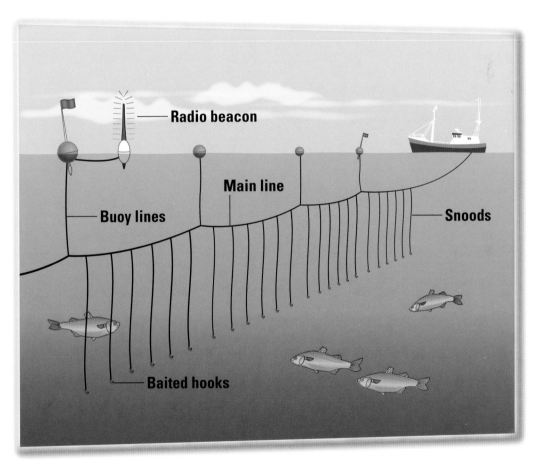

The largest longlines may have up
to 2,500 baited hooks.

How commercial fishers catch fish and seafood

Fishing Method	Percent Using the Method	How It Works
Trawl	50%	Dragging a net along the seafloor or through the water; used for shrimp, anchovies, mackerel, squid, and rockfish
Purse Seine	25%	Using a net that can be pulled closed to trap the fish; used for sardines, mackerel, herring, tuna, and salmon
Pot and Trap	7%	Setting baited wooden or metal traps on the seafloor; used for lobsters, crabs, and crayfish
Longline	5%	Pulling a very long line with many individual baited hooks behind a ship; used for swordfish, tuna, sablefish, and halibut
Gillnet	3%	Using nets that fish can only partially fit through that catches fish by the gills; used mostly for salmon
Dredge	less than 2%	Using a large, rake-like scraper to scoop shellfish off the sea bottom; used for oysters or scallops
Pole/Troll	less than 1%	Using a long pole with a hook to catch individual fish and haul them on a ship; used for mahimahi and some types of tuna

Pole and troll

Some fish, such as mahimahi and certain types of tuna, are caught one at a time using poles or trolls. Fishers use long poles with hooks to snag each fish and haul it onto the ship. The hooks do not have **barbs** on them, so the fish slip off the hooks easily.

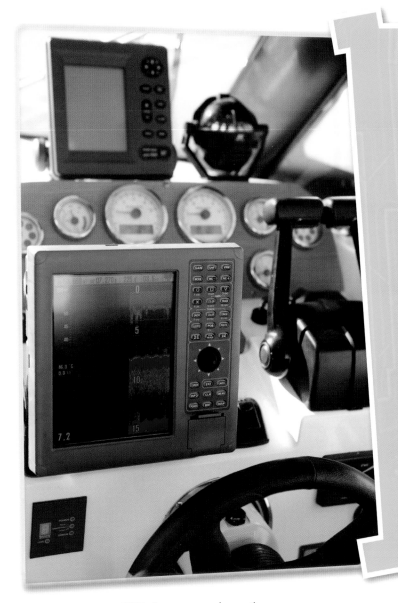

GPS devices such as this one are used in some fishing boats.

GPS Fishfinders

Up until recently, commercial fishing was a hit-or-miss process. Fishers had to follow seabirds or guess where they would find schools of fish. Many days fishers returned to port with a poor catch. Today fishers use **Global Positioning System (GPS)** fishfinders. The technology uses **sonar** to find schools of fish. The GPS bounces sound off the seafloor. If there are schools of fish in the water, the sound bounces off the fish. GPS allows fishers to catch more fish.

Is Commercial Fishing Safe?

Commercial fishing is one of the most dangerous jobs in the world. Foul weather, high waves, and problems with machines lead to serious accidents. When the fishing **vessel** is heaving under high waves, fishers run the risk of being washed overboard. There is also a chance that intense cold will produce frostbite on hands and feet. And because of the intense machinery and slippery, wet conditions there is a chance for accidents.

Safety measures

Laws are in place to keep fishers safe. Workers who go out on a rolling deck put on **inflatable** vests in case they get washed over the side. The vests hook onto a safety line that is linked to a secure anchor. Both the vest and waterproof suits fishers wear are glow-in-the-dark yellow or orange. If an accident does happen, rescue crews will be able to see the missing person.

There is always a danger of being swept overboard on fishing vessels. Top-of-the-line inflatable vests are designed to save lives. They have lights and give off signals to help rescuers find a person that has been washed into the sea.

In many places crews take safety courses and must get certificates to show that they passed the courses. They learn how to handle emergencies, such as fires on a ship, and ways to use rescue equipment. Some companies also insist that commercial fishers learn CPR (cardiopulmonary resuscitation) techniques. Crews need to know what to do to keep their fellow fishers safe.

Winter winds in the Bering Sea can reach 80 knots (about 90 miles per hour or 145 kilometers per hour).

What Is Aquaculture?

Aquaculture is the business of farming fish, shellfish, and marine plants. Common farmed fish species include striped bass, carp, tilapia, catfish, trout, and salmon. Australia, the Philippines, Japan, and South Africa farm oysters. Italy, Spain, and France raise blue mussels. Worldwide the most commonly farmed aquaculture product is carp. Thailand, China, and Vietnam are active shrimp farming countries. China and Japan lead the world in farming seaweed, including nori and kelp, which are eaten as food.

Most salmon sold in supermarkets is from farm-raised fish.

Aquaculture began in China about 4,000 years ago and in Egypt during the Middle Kingdom (2052–1786 BCE). Modern fish farming, similar to today's industry, was first developed in Germany in 1773. It did not become popular until about 1970. Between 1970 and 1975, the aquaculture business doubled in the amount of food it produced. Today fish is the main protein food source for more than one billion people. It accounts for 7.5 percent of the food produced in the world.

More than just food

Fish farming affects several industries. Scientists and engineers develop improved methods for aquaculture. Farmers need to feed their fish and shellfish, so people have jobs producing the food. Other people build ponds or the equipment used to move water into and out of the ponds. Aquaculture products may be used to make **fertilizer** and **pharmaceuticals**, as well as gelatin, ice cream, and toothpaste.

Dr. Modadugu V. Gupta (born 1939)

In 2005 the World Food Prize honored Modadugu Gupta for being a prime designer of the "blue revolution" in Asia. The blue revolution finds ways to farm fish in unlikely places, such as rice paddies. The ability to harvest rice and shrimp or tilapia from one rice paddy is perfect—two foodstuffs from one basic source.

Setting up a fish farm

Farming fish requires a good deal of planning. A fish farm must have the right climate and plenty of clean water. Fish farms can create serious **pollution** problems if the water is not filtered and disposed of properly. Equipment for handling water must be chosen carefully. A fish farm, like an aquarium, will smell of fish if it is not properly cared for, and neighbors may object.

A fish farm needs several different levels of pens or ponds, so the farm takes up plenty of space. The **hatchery** is where the fish eggs hatch into **fry**. The fry move into a **nursery** to grow larger before being transferred into a growth pond. The fish and seafood need to be carefully watched to control the spread of diseases or **parasites**. Harvested fish need to be processed for sale and shipped to buyers.

Pens, cages, and ponds

Farming fish is not a one-method-fits-all business. The type of equipment used depends on the species of fish being farmed. Salmon and tuna are generally raised in open net pens or cages along a seacoast or in freshwater lakes. Inland or coastal ponds are used for growing shrimp, catfish, and tilapia. Rainbow trout are often grown in raceways. A raceway redirects water from a stream or well through a fish-holding area and back into the main water source. **Recirculating** ponds, used for striped bass and sturgeon, filter the water and return it back to the pond.

Whether fish farms use pens, cages, or ponds, problems arise. The fish produce waste that can pollute local water sources. Setting up a fish farm may cause damage to the **environment**. Building shrimp farms in Southeast Asia has destroyed coastal mangroves, which are tropical trees that grow in marshy coastal regions. Mangroves are not only natural fish nurseries, they also protect against storm damage and soil erosion. Aquaculture needs to find a balance between producing fish for **profit** and saving the environment.

This fish farm is divided into more than one section.

Can We Farm Fish in the Ocean?

Currently offshore farming is commonly used for raising salmon. Large pens are built in bays or estuaries, which are the waters at the mouth of a river. The pens look like large playpens that are open on the top. The pens float from an anchor. Netting prevents the fish from escaping but allows water to flow through the pen.

These fishing pens are located on a farm on the northwest coast of Scotland.

Open-ocean pens are anchored to the seafloor, but they float with ocean currents.

Net Pens

An open-seas net pen is either a cube-shaped or ball-shaped system for open-ocean **aquaculture**. It works well in rough seas and can be anchored to the seafloor. Workers can access the pods for feeding, transferring fish, or harvesting. The mesh design keeps fish in but allows water to flow through the pod easily. The water's action keeps the pod clean of fish waste materials. Predators, such as sharks, cannot bite through the pod's reinforced grid. So far, experiments in open-ocean farming have been successful.

Water flow removes waste from the pen. However, bays have calm waters, and it is possible to pollute a bay with waste from farmed fish. Norway is the leading producer of farmed salmon, growing one-third of the world's supply. Chile, Scotland, and Canada also have major offshore fish farms. **Conservationists** have serious concerns about **pollution** in these countries and other nations that have offshore fish farming.

Farming seaweed

Seaweed is a popular food item in northern Europe and Asia and is seeing increased popularity in the United States and Canada. Dulse, nori, kelp, and laver are seaweed species eaten in Japan, China, Iceland, Ireland, Wales, and other countries. Seaweed is easy to grow and harvest. It can be processed into sheets, rolls, and pills. Seaweed is also an ingredient in brownie mixes, infant formulas, margarine, yogurt, and ice cream.

Some African nations have begun farming seaweed as a good source of protein.

Aquaculture and the environment

Nature provides a natural balance among species in a **fishery**. Water pollution and overfishing destroy that balance. The species that live within a fishery may die off or be fished to **extinction**. Aquaculture methods are being used to reintroduce fish and shellfish in order to return bays and rivers to their natural state.

Chesapeake Bay oysters

Chesapeake Bay, Maryland, suffered from overfishing of oysters and water pollution. The aquaculture technique of **seeding** oysters, or developing new oyster beds, has been part of a major program to renew the bay. Oysters are filter feeders. They suck in water and pieces of plant and animal matter, eating the matter and spitting clean water out. They also attract fish and crustaceans that feed on the oysters. The Chesapeake Bay is on its way to complete recovery.

River pollution

England's Tyne River suffered from serious pollution. Conservationists developed a program to clean the water. Once that was accomplished, the next step was to restock fish populations. The program has returned salmon to the river. Aquaculture specialists introduced salmon eggs, called roe, upstream in the Tyne. Salmon hatch from eggs, grow, and swim downstream to an ocean. They live in the ocean until they have the urge to produce young, and then they return to the stream where they were born. Adult salmon are now returning to the river each year.

How Does Fish Get from the Sea to the Supermarket?

When restaurants advertise their "Catch of the Day," they are usually telling the truth. Small fishing **vessels** put fish on ice as soon as it is caught. Packed in ice, the fish stays fresh until the vessel returns to port. The fish go directly from the ship to a market. Buyers arrive at the market early to get the best fish for the best price. They ship fresh fish by train, truck, or plane to fish markets, supermarkets, or restaurant supply companies.

Frozen fish is processed in different ways depending on the company that sells the fish. Some fish-packing companies have their own vessels that fish for them. Others hire privately owned fishing vessels or arrange to buy all of a ship's catch when the vessel comes into port. The fish are taken to a processing plant, which is usually close to the port. At the plant, the fish meat is cleaned, prepared, packaged, and frozen or canned. It is then shipped to supermarkets.

Floating factories

When fish leave the sea, they begin to spoil. To keep fish at its freshest, some companies build floating processing factories. The fish go from the sea to the freezer in only a couple of hours. The fish are hauled on board in huge nets. Fish are sorted by species, size, and quality. Then the fish move into the processing part of the ship. The fish are cleaned, prepared, and packaged immediately. The ships have huge freezers to hold the processed fish or seafood. A fish factory ship can stay at sea for weeks at a time. When freezers are full, the ship returns to port. Floating fish factories ensure top-quality frozen fish on supermarket shelves.

People who work on floating fish factories live on the ship for many weeks.

Who Buys and Sells the Most Fish?

The market value of world fish and seafood products rises every year. According to the Food and Agriculture Organization (FAO), about 38 percent of all fish caught worldwide is traded internationally. Half of the exported fish in the world is caught or farmed in developing countries. Japan, the United States, Canada, and the European Union buy 80 percent of that exported fish.

There are more than 43 million people worldwide who work as **commercial** fishers or run fish farms. Many others make and supply fishing equipment, food for farmed fish, or equipment for processing fish. Still others process and sell fish. The top 10 seafood producers are China, Peru, Japan, the United States, Chile, Indonesia, India, Thailand, Norway, and Iceland.

This map shows the amount of fish in tons each country produced in the year 2002.

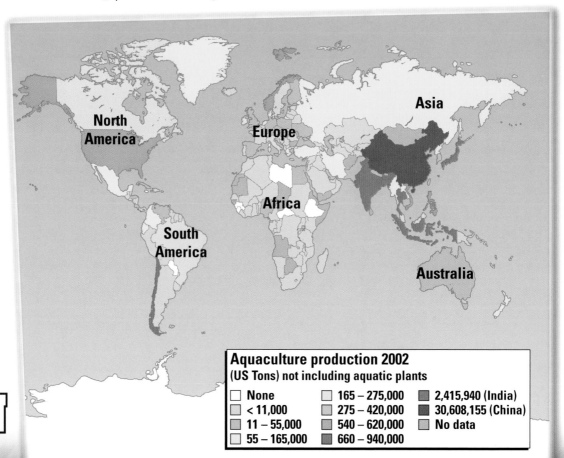

North America

Europe

Asia

Africa

South America

Australia

Aquaculture production 2002
(US Tons) not including aquatic plants

☐ None	☐ 165 – 275,000	▨ 2,415,940 (India)
☐ < 11,000	☐ 275 – 420,000	■ 30,608,155 (China)
▨ 11 – 55,000	▨ 540 – 620,000	☐ No data
☐ 55 – 165,000	■ 660 – 940,000	

A fisher covers fish with ice in Iceland.

Imports and exports

The largest single exporter of fish is China. Much of this fish and seafood is produced through **aquaculture**. Today's aquaculture market is dominated by China, Thailand, the Philippines, and Vietnam. Asia-Pacific producers account for 87 percent of aquaculture products worldwide.

The three biggest importers of fish and seafood are Japan, the United States, and Europe, which together account for 70 percent of all fish imports. Japan is the largest single national importer, and the amount Japan imports will increase over the next few years. The 2011 earthquake and tsunami that struck Japan have affected aquaculture and local **fisheries**. To feed its people, Japan will need to import more fish and seafood.

Slowing growth

Aquaculture growth is slowing, even though new regions have joined the aquaculture market. In the past 40 years, Latin America and the Caribbean have shown the highest average annual growth at just over 20 percent. Latin American and Caribbean products include Chilean salmon, tilapia, cobia, and shrimp. Africa is also becoming an aquaculture power with 12.6 percent growth. West African countries raise Nile tilapia, catfish, ningu, and common carp. Farther to the south, countries also farm mussels, abalone, prawns, and oysters. The increase in aquaculture in these developing regions is important for growing regional economies.

Oysters are raised on this farm in South Africa.

When commercial fishers could no longer fish cod, many could not pay their bills and lost their boats due to debt.

Case Study: The World Market for Cod

For many years, cod was the most popular fish species on dinner tables. It was the main ingredient in fish-and-chips, used to make fish sticks, and served in restaurants. By the early 1990s, governments realized that the Atlantic cod fishery had been fished nearly to **extinction**. Fishing for Atlantic cod became illegal.

Many commercial fishers depended on cod to make a living. The new law put them out of business. Others tried fishing for species that lived farther out to sea. Their boats were not sturdy enough for deep-ocean fishing. The number of accidents and at-sea rescues increased at tremendous cost.

Scientists expected that, after a few years, the cod fishery would return to large numbers, but it has not. Pressure from commercial fishers reopened cod fishing in 2004 with quotas to control how much fish was caught. However, the catch remains low, and the Atlantic cod population has not even returned to half the numbers that swam the North Atlantic in the 1960s. Most of the cod we eat today is caught in the Pacific Ocean.

How Can We Preserve Fisheries?

Here are some facts about human abuse of the sea's bounty. Major fishing efforts began in the 11th century. By the 14th century, several European species of fish, such as plaice, already showed signs of overfishing.

The 18th century saw the rise of whaling and sealing, with little concern for the future. The end result was that 12 whale species and 4 seal and sea lion species are now endangered (at risk of becoming **extinct**).

What happened with whales and seals is now happening to many ocean fish species. Overfishing has reduced the populations to the point that many species would not recover even if all fishing of these species stopped immediately. The most overfished species include Atlantic cod, swordfish, orange roughy, red snapper, several types of tuna, Alaska pollock, and Atlantic halibut.

Sustainable fisheries

There are no longer plenty of fish in the sea. The biggest problems are overfishing and the growing demand for more fish. **Conservation** groups say that the answer to overfishing is **sustainable fisheries**. A sustainable fishery simply means that fishers have to stop taking fish faster than the fish can **reproduce**.

Better fishing practices

Sustainable fisheries ensure that fishing considers all species within an **ecosystem**. Catching tuna, for example, should not be done with nets that also catch and kill dolphins. Quality fishery management protects sensitive marine species, such as whales and seals. It is important to maintain stocks of specific species at population levels that allow a species to reproduce successfully. Loss of a species, such as Atlantic cod, is not acceptable. The natural balance of oceans depends on a wide range of healthy fish populations.

Too many dolphins get tangled in nets meant for catching tuna.

Guillermo Alvarez

Guillermo Alvarez has been promoting sea conservation for more than 40 years. He works to repair the damage done by fishing with **gillnets** in Mexico's Sea of Cortez. Gillnets depleted Mexico's white sea bass and tuna fisheries. Today Alvarez, a marine scientist, opposes the use of gillnets, longlines, and heavy bottom **trawling.** These fishing methods, he believes, kill many more bycatch species than the species fishers want to catch. Alvarez feels these fishing methods reduce fisheries well below sustainable levels.

Protecting endangered species

Commercial fishing often collects a certain amount of **bycatch**. Bycatch is fish, birds, or mammals that were not supposed to be caught in the fishing nets. Commercial fishing endangers sharks, sea turtles, dolphins, and seabirds such as albatrosses. Sea turtles and dolphins need to breathe air, and they drown in fishing nets. Seabirds searching for food go after bait on **longline** hooks. They get caught and dragged underwater. New technology protects endangered species and still allows fishers to catch fish.

TEDs: Turtle Excluder Devices

Turtle excluder devices (TEDs) are grids of bars with openings that allow turtles to escape from the top or bottom of a fish net. TEDs are used mainly on shrimp trawlers. When turtles, or even sharks, get caught and strike the grids, they are ejected from the nets.

By using TEDs (see box), fishers can catch shrimp
and allow endangered sea turtles to go free.

Can We Produce Enough Fish to Feed the World?

There are approximately 200 types of fish harvested around the world. Of those 200 species, about 50 are overfished. It is important to find a balance between the human need for fish and seafood and maintaining healthy oceans. Overfishing destroys the natural balance of the oceans and seas.

Hans Jusseit

After years in **commercial** fishing, Australian Hans Jusseit developed the Smart Hook. This is a device that is added onto **longline** hooks to make them sink quickly. The hook's design prevents seabirds and sea turtles from getting hooked on the lines. **Conservation** groups, such as the Southern Seabird Solutions Alliance, have honored Jusseit for his invention.

To enforce fishing laws, government agencies need fishing **vessels** to be licensed. Fishers that fail to follow the rules could be fined or barred from fishing. Unfortunately, governments can only set rules for their own waters, which range up to 200 miles (320 kilometers) from the coastline. The oceans are huge, and large areas are considered international waters. A government cannot enforce laws outside the waters in its own territory.

Even a small fishing vessel should not take fish listed as overfished.

Fishing quotas are set by government agencies. Quotas limit the amount of a species that can be caught or the time period, called a season, when fishing that species is legal. For example, Iceland called a halt to capelin fishing when the species population dropped too low. Quotas are hard to put into effect. Fishers can take an illegal catch and then sell and offload it at sea. They can catch fish within a nation's waters and then head to international waters, where that nation has no control. It is hard to check every fishing vessel or catch to make sure that quotas are followed.

Meeting demands

In the past 50 years, **aquaculture** has been both good and bad for people and the planet. The main problems of aquaculture stem from **pollution** and loss of coastal habitats.

On the other hand, aquaculture has provided an increased protein supply for developing countries, along with jobs that did not exist 50 years ago. For example, Kolkata, India, has fish farms that produce 13,000 tons (11,793 metric tons) of food for the city's inhabitants. The fish feed on 159 million gallons (600 million liters) of raw sewage from the city's sewer system. Workers earn money harvesting and processing the fish for sale in local markets.

Destroying wetlands

In Southeast Asia shrimp farms have been built along coasts, destroying natural wetlands that serve as nature's filter against pollution. The loss of wetlands also reduces the amount of wild fish, shellfish, and crustaceans in the oceans. Many species use wetlands for laying eggs and as a safe area for young to grow.

Genetically modified fish

In nature the characteristics of a species are passed from one generation to the next through **genes**. Over a long time, a species may develop genes that allow for greater growth, more flesh, or longer life.

Today scientists take genes for certain characteristics and use those genes to produce **hybrids** of a species. These new species are called genetically modified (GM) species. With salmon, scientists took genes from the ocean pout, which is an eel-like fish, and changed the characteristics of the salmon. The new "super" salmon grows much faster than its wild relatives.

Science may provide the solutions that will add protein to people's diets and jobs for workers in the seafood industry. Aquaculture is expanding to produce larger quantities and more varieties of fish, shellfish, and crustaceans for us to eat. The rich harvest that once came from the seas will come from fish farms in the future.

In this photo, you can see the difference in size between a genetically modified salmon and its wild cousin.

Glossary

aquaculture process of farming fish, seafood, or marine plants

barb sharp, pointed tip on a hook

bycatch incidental fish caught along with the target species

clan group of families that are related to each other or share a common aim

commercial done for business purposes

conservation protection, preservation, or management of a species or habitat

conservationist person who works to protect, preserve, or manage a species

drogue drum that acts like a drag to slow down a fleeing whale

ecosystem system of living things and their environment

environment all of the living and nonliving elements that affect the organisms living in an area

evidence valid and reliable proof collected through observations or measurements made of data collected over time

extinct having no individuals of a species still alive

fertilizer substance that nourishes or feeds plants

fishery place where fish or shellfish are caught

flax natural plant fiber used to make linen

fry tiny fish that are newly hatched from their eggs

gauge standard measurement of space within openings in a net

gene basic unit through which animals and plants inherit specific characteristics

gillnet net with wide opening that catches fish by their gills

Global Positioning System (GPS) electronic device that calculates the location of a place or thing using information from satellites

harpoon large, heavy spear used for whale hunting

hatchery place for hatching fish eggs

hybrid new species that results from crossing genes from two different animal or plant species

inflatable able to be blown up and hold air

longline long central line from which many hooks hang

midden garbage dump from prehistoric times

Neanderthal prehistoric human relative who lived from 125,000 years ago to about 24,000 years ago

nursery place to raise young

parasite organism that feeds from another living thing and may live on or in it

pharmaceuticals medicinal drugs

pollution introduction of harmful substances into the air, soil, or water

profit money or income gained

purse seine long, wall-like net that can be pulled into a purse

recirculating flowing through a system repeatedly

reproduce have young of a species

seeding sew or scatter the embryos of oysters to start an oyster bed

sonar method for detecting and locating objects underwater

sustainable way of using natural resources that also conserves them for future use

technological to do with using machines as part of life, society, or work

trawl heavy net that is dragged along the seafloor to scoop up shrimp; also the act of using such a net

vessel ship

Find Out More

Books

Boudreau, Helene. *Life in a Fishing Community*. New York: Crabtree, 2009.

Inskipp, Carol. *Healthy Seas*. Mankato, Minn.: Smart Apple Media, 2007.

Lourie, Peter. *Whaling Season: A Year in the Life of an Arctic Whale Scientist*. Boston: Houghton Mifflin, 2009.

Moore, Heidi. *Ocean Food Chains*. Chicago: Heinemann Library, 2011.

Somervill, Barbara A. *Commercial Fisher*. Ann Arbor, Mich.: Cherry Lake, 2011.

Tieck, Sarah. *Commercial Fishermen*. Edina, Minn.: ABDO, 2012.

Williams, Dinah. *Shocking Seafood*. New York: Bearport, 2009.

Websites

The Alaska Seafood Marking Institute (ASMI)

The Alaska Seafood Marking Institute (ASMI) is the "go-to" site for fish and seafood caught in Alaska's waters. They offer everything from information on sustainable fisheries to recipes for fish tacos.

www.alaskaseafood.org

Columbia River History

The Columbia River has an ancient heritage of commercial fishing. American Indians fished and traded salmon for centuries along the river. Learn more about this interesting heritage.

www.nwcouncil.org/history/commercialfishing.asp

The World Wildlife Fund (WWF)

Almost half of the seafood we eat comes from farms, making aquaculture an economic opportunity and a concern. The World Wildlife Fund (WWF) offers aquaculture information.

www.worldwildlife.org/aquaculture/

Places to visit

Fisheries Museum of the Atlantic
68 Bluenose Drive
Lunenburg, Nova Scotia, Canada B0J 2C0
866-579-4909

http://museum.gov.ns.ca/fma/en/home/default.aspx

Maritime Museum of San Diego
1492 North Harbor Drive
San Diego, CA 92101
619-234-9153

www.sdmaritime.org/

Mystic Seaport Museum
75 Greenmanville Avenue
Mystic, CT 06355
888-973-2767

www.mysticseaport.org

New Bedford Whaling Museum
18 Johnny Cake Hill
New Bedford, MA 02740
508-997-0046

www.whalingmuseum.org

Index